THE COMPLETE WOOD PELLET SMOKER AND GRILL COOKBOOK 2020

THE ULTIMATE GUIDE AND RECIPE BOOK FOR WOOD PELLET GRILLS USE THIS GUIDE FOR SMOKING MEAT, FISH, GAME, AND VEGETABLES

CONTENTS

Introduction

Through history, smoking been a preferred way of preserving food, but it so much more than just a way to keep food from going bad! Smoking also introduces complex and delicious flavors into dishes that are otherwise often bland or uninteresting. In modern cooking, it's a great way to mix up staples in your home cooking, and it can be a really fantastic way to wow people at a potluck, or to host an incredible dinner party. Smoking is not only inventive and delicious, it also makes it really easy to make large quantities of food at the same time without too much fuss. Traditionally, smoking is done by burning wood chips in a small enclosed area with the food, allowing the food to be cooked very slowly, while absorbing the rich smoky flavor. Today, smoking is often associated with sports tail-gaiting parties and small family get-togethers. This guide is designed to both embrace that culture, and also offer up some techniques and recipes that will let you take your smoking to the next level: full-blown gourmet food full of layered and nuanced deliciousness.

Chapter 1: Beef Recipes

Smoked Ribeye Steaks

PREP TIME: 15 MINUTES

COOKING TIME: 35 MINUTES

SERVINGS: 1 PERSON

NUTRITIONAL VALUE (ESTIMATED AMOUNT PER SERVING)
517 Calories   341 Calories from Fat   38g Total Fat   17g Saturated Fat   1.8g Polyunsaturated Fat   18g Monounsaturated Fat   154mg Cholesterol   118mg Sodium   558mg Potassium   0.3g Total Carbohydrates   0g Dietary Fiber   0g Sugars   44g Protein

INGREDIENTS
- ½ pound Ribeye steaks, preferably 2" thick; at room temperature for half an hour
- Steak rub, any of your favorite

DIRECTIONS
1. Preheat wood-pellet grill over low smoke. Sprinkle the ribeye steaks with the desired steak rub
2. Place the coated Ribeye on wood-pellet grill & let smoke for 20 to 25 minutes
3. Once done; remove the meat from grill; adjusting the temperature of pellet grill to 400 F
4. Place the ribeye over the pellet grill again & sear each side for a couple of 5 minutes.

5. Continue to cook the meat until you get your desired doneness (Steak at 165 F is considered to be well done, 145 F is considered to be medium, and 125 F is considered to be rare). It's important for you to pull off the steak from the grill approximately 5 degrees before the desired temp. Wrap in aluminum foil & let sit for a couple of minutes then slice into pieces. Serve hot and enjoy

Balsamic Soy Flank Steak Recipe

PREP TIME: 20 MINUTES

COOKING TIME: 30 MINUTES

SERVINGS: 4 PERSONS

NUTRITIONAL VALUE (ESTIMATED AMOUNT PER SERVING)
423 Calories   235 Calories from Fat   26g Total Fat   7g Saturated Fat   0g
Trans Fat   2g Polyunsaturated Fat   15g Monounsaturated Fat   111mg
Cholesterol   1603mg Sodium   701mg Potassium   7.1g Total Carbohydrates
1.1g Dietary Fiber   3.4g Sugars   38g Protein

INGREDIENTS
- 1½ pounds flank steak
- 3 cloves garlic, chopped
- ½ onion, chopped
- 1 tablespoon Dijon mustard
- ½ teaspoon black pepper
- 1 tablespoon dried rosemary
- ¼ cup each of olive oil, balsamic vinegar & soy sauce
- 1 teaspoon salt

DIRECTIONS
1. For Soy Balsamic Marinade: Whisk the garlic with onion, balsamic vinegar, olive oil, soy sauce, rosemary, Dijon, pepper and salt in a large-sized mixing bowl.
2. Place the steak in a large sized zip-lock bag; add the prepared marinade. Seal the bag & shake the ingredients well (ensure that the meat pieces are nicely coated with the prepared marinade). Place the bag in a refrigerator for overnight.
3. The next day; preheat your wood-pellet grill to 350 F in advance.

4. Once done; remove the steak from bag; shake off any excess marinade (reserving the excess marinade in the bag for later use).

5. Place the coated steak on the grill & cook until you get your desired doneness, for several minutes on each side. As you are cooking the meat; don't forget to brush the pieces with the kept-aside marinade. Once done; remove the steak from grill & let rest for 5 minutes on a cutting board. Thinly cut the grilled steak across the grain. Serve hot and enjoy.

Beef Tenderloin With Balsamic Glaze

PREP TIME: 20 MINUTES

COOKING TIME: 1 HOUR & 20 MINUTES

SERVINGS: 4 PERSONS

NUTRITIONAL VALUE (ESTIMATED AMOUNT PER SERVING)
802 Calories   439 Calories from Fat   49g Total Fat   23g Saturated Fat   0.5g Trans Fat   1.9g Polyunsaturated Fat   19g Monounsaturated Fat   150mg Cholesterol   224mg Sodium   778mg Potassium   49g Total Carbohydrates 0.3g Dietary Fiber   44g Sugars   32g Protein

INGREDIENTS
- 1 ½ pounds beef tenderloin; trimmed, silver skin removed
- Beef rub, as required; any of your favorite

FOR BALSAMIC REDUCTION
- 3 cups balsamic vinegar
- 3 tablespoons rosemary, fresh, finely chopped
- 1/3 cup brown sugar
- 3-4 tablespoons softened butter, at room temperature
- 3 garlic cloves; peeled & crushed
- Pepper & salt, to taste

DIRECTIONS
1. For evenly cooking; fold the tail (chain portion) over & secure it with toothpicks or butcher's twine then, season with your favorite beef rub.
2. Set your wood pellet smoker grill to 250 F in advance. Once done; cook the tenderloin until the meat reflects an internal temperature of 110 to 115 F, for an hour, preferably on the bottom rack. Remove the meat & let rest. In the meantime; set your grill temperature to 500 F. Once done; place the partially

cooked tenderloin on the searing rack and cook until the meat reflects an internal temperature of 130 F, for a minute on each side.

3. Remove the tenderloin & place it on a clean, large-sized cutting board & rest for a couple of minutes before cutting. Slice into desired strips. Serve immediately; drizzled with the prepared balsamic reduction on top & enjoy.

FOR BALSAMIC REDUCTION

1. Over moderate heat in a large saucepan; combine the entire ingredients together until mixed well, for a couple of minutes.

Butter Beef Tenderloin

PREP TIME: 20 MINUTES

COOKING TIME: 55 MINUTES

SERVINGS: 8 PERSONS

NUTRITIONAL VALUE (ESTIMATED AMOUNT PER SERVING)
891 Calories   666 Calories from Fat   74g Total Fat   33g Saturated Fat   0.5g Trans Fat   3.1g Polyunsaturated Fat   30g Monounsaturated Fat   229mg Cholesterol   513mg Sodium   900mg Potassium   1.4g Total Carbohydrates   0.4g Dietary Fiber   0.3g Sugars   52g Protein

INGREDIENTS
- 4 to 5 pounds beef tenderloin
- 2 tablespoons Worcestershire sauce
- ½ cup softened butter, at room temperature
- 2 teaspoons fresh rosemary, finely chopped
- 4 garlic cloves, minced
- 2 tablespoons course ground mustard
- 1 teaspoon each of black pepper & kosher salt

DIRECTIONS
1. Preheat your wood pellet grill to high heat in advance.
2. Cream the butter with Worcestershire sauce, garlic, rosemary, mustard, pepper and salt in a large-sized mixing bowl.
3. Pat the tenderloin dry & cover them with the prepared butter mixture completely; pressing the pieces softly into the mixture to adhere.
4. Let stand for half an hour at room temperature and then, place the coated tenderloin over the hot grill grate.

5. Roast for 15 minutes on high-heat; decrease the temperature to high smoke & smoke until you get your desired doneness, internal temperature should reflect somewhere 130 F.
6. Remove from the pellet grill & let stand for 7 to 10 minutes then slice into desired pieces.

Smoke-Roasted Beef Tenderloin

PREP TIME: 20 MINUTES

COOKING TIME: 1 HOUR & 20 MINUTES

SERVINGS: 8 PERSONS

NUTRITIONAL VALUE (ESTIMATED AMOUNT PER SERVING)
652 Calories   476 Calories from Fat   53g Total Fat   21g Saturated Fat   0g Trans Fat   2.3g Polyunsaturated Fat   23g Monounsaturated Fat   159mg Cholesterol   111mg Sodium   693mg Potassium   0.2g Total Carbohydrates   0.1g Dietary Fiber   0g Sugars   41g Protein

INGREDIENTS
- 1 whole beef tenderloin, trimmed (roughly 4 pounds)
- 1 to 2 tablespoons extra virgin olive oil, plus more for basting
- Freshly ground or cracked black pepper
- Vegetable oil, for oiling the rack
- Coarse salt or smoked salt (kosher or sea)

DIRECTIONS
1. Set up your wood pellet smoker & preheat it to 225 F to 250 F in advance.
2. Place the meat on a large-sized rimmed baking sheet & generously season with pepper and salt on all sides. Next, drizzle the tenderloin with olive oil on all sides, rubbing well.
3. Place the coated tenderloin on the smoker & smoke for 45 to 60 minutes, until the internal temperature of the meat reflects 110 F. Transfer it to a large platter & let rest for a couple of minutes.
4. In the meantime, set up your grill & preheat to high (for direct grilling). Brush & oil the grill grate.
5. Transfer the tenderloin to the hot grill. Direct grill for a couple of minutes, until all sides are dark, crusty, and sizzling and the internal temperature of

the meat reflects 130 to 135 F (for medium-rare) or 120 to 125 F (for rare beef); rotating the meat like a log. As it grills; don't forget to brush the cooked tenderloin with more of olive oil & turning the pieces halfway during the grilling process until grill marks appear.

6. Place the cooked tenderloin on a clean, large-sized cutting board & get rid of the strings. Cut the meat crosswise into ¼ to ½" thick slices.

Chapter 2: Pork Recipes

Smoked Pork Belly

PREP TIME: 15 MINUTES

COOKING TIME: 4 HOURS & 15 MINUTES

SERVINGS: 10 PERSONS

NUTRITIONAL VALUE (ESTIMATED AMOUNT PER SERVING)
1175 Calories   1082 Calories from Fat   120g Total Fat   44g Saturated Fat   0g Trans Fat   13g Polyunsaturated Fat   56g Monounsaturated Fat   163mg Cholesterol   73mg Sodium   425mg Potassium   0.1g Total Carbohydrates   0.1g Dietary Fiber   0g Sugars   21g Protein

INGREDIENTS
- 3 to 5 pounds pork belly
- Smoked paprika, pepper & salt to taste

DIRECTIONS
1. Preheat your pellet grill over high smoke.
2. Once done; score the fat cap then, generously season with smoked paprika, pepper & salt.
3. Smoke for 4 hours, until the internal temperature of meat reflects 165 F.
4. Remove the cooked meat from grill & let rest for 8 to 10 minutes then, cut into individual portions; serve hot and enjoy.

Delicious Pork Sandwich

PREP TIME: 20 MINUTES

COOKING TIME: 12 HOURS & 30 MINUTES

SERVINGS: 8 PERSONS

NUTRITIONAL VALUE (ESTIMATED AMOUNT PER SERVING)
607 Calories   400 Calories from Fat   44g Total Fat   21g Saturated Fat   0.6g Trans Fat   2.9g Polyunsaturated Fat   15g Monounsaturated Fat   179mg Cholesterol   1288mg Sodium   744mg Potassium   1.4g Total Carbohydrates   0g Dietary Fiber   0.1g Sugars   50g Protein

INGREDIENTS

FOR THE CUBAN SANDWICH
- 1 ½ pounds roasted pork, sliced
- 1 pound Swiss cheese, sliced
- 1 ½ pounds deli ham, sliced
- Dill pickles, sliced lengthwise
- 8 Cuban rolls, sliced lengthwise
- ½ stick unsalted butter, softened
- 3 tablespoons yellow mustard or more to taste

FOR THE ROASTED PORK
- 6-8 pounds boneless pork shoulder
- 2 heads of garlic, roughly chopped
- 2 2/3 cups lime juice
- 2 onions, cut into rings
- 1 tablespoon cumin
- 2 tablespoons oregano
- 4 cups orange juice
- 1 tablespoon black pepper
- 3 tablespoons salt

DIRECTIONS

FOR THE ROASTED PORK
1. Combine the entire ingredients (don't add the pork shoulder) in a large-sized mixing bowl. Season the pork butt with pepper and salt; cover the meat with the prepared marinade. Cover & let refrigerate for overnight.
2. The next day; remove the pork butt & place them in high sided pan or casserole dish. Strain the marinade & add the liquid to the meat.
3. Smoke until meat reflects the internal temperature as 205 F, for 10 to 12 hours, at high smoke.
4. Remove the pork butt & let rest then, pull the pork apart.

FOR THE SANDWICHES
1. Evenly spread the mustard on the roll, on both sides. Add the cooked pork and then, add cheese, ham & pickle. Top with top bun & then, wrap in an aluminum foil. Place the wrapped sandwiches over a grill; grill for a couple of minutes, until the cheese is completely melted, over medium heat; pressing the sandwiches with a cast iron skillet.
2. Get rid of the foil & butter the sandwich on both sides. Place it over the grill again & brown each side until you get your desired level of doneness then, remove from the grill & enjoy.

Smoked Pork Ribs

PREP TIME: 20 MINUTES

COOKING TIME: 6 HOURS & 20 MINUTES

SERVINGS: 6 PERSONS

NUTRITIONAL VALUE (ESTIMATED AMOUNT PER SERVING)
595 Calories   323 Calories from Fat   36g Total Fat   13g Saturated Fat   0.3g Trans Fat   5.9g Polyunsaturated Fat   15g Monounsaturated Fat   146mg Cholesterol   719mg Sodium   597mg Potassium   24g Total Carbohydrates   0.9g Dietary Fiber   19g Sugars   42g Protein

INGREDIENTS
- 3 racks baby back ribs
- 1 ½ tablespoon mustard
- BBQ Rub, any of your favorite
- 1 ½ tablespoon maple syrup
- ½ cup apple juice
- Coarse salt

FOR GLAZE
- 1 cup ketchup
- ½ cup maple syrup
- 3 tablespoons hot sauce
- 1 teaspoon pepper
- 3 tablespoons vinegar
- ½ cup mustard

DIRECTIONS

1. Rinse the ribs & then, patting them dry using a paper towel. Score the silver skin (membrane) on the concave side of the ribs; peel it off using a paper towel. Generously season the ribs with salt and then, let the brine to dry for an hour.

2. Combine the apple juice with maple syrup and mustard in a spray bottle. Combine the entire glaze ingredients together in a medium sized bowl; set the mixture aside until ready to use.

3. Preheat your pellet grill with high smoke. Once you have brined the ribs have for one hour; spritz them with the prepared mixture in the spray bottle. Cover the ribs completely with the prepared rub & put them in a smoker; cook for 3 hours. Once done; spread the glaze on top of the ribs & cover them in an aluminum foil; continue to smoke for 2 more hours. Get rid of the foil & cook for an hour; don't forget to spread some more glaze on top of the meat. Serve hot and enjoy.

Smoked Braided Pork Loin

PREP TIME: 20 MINUTES

COOKING TIME: 2 HOURS & 55 MINUTES

SERVINGS: 8 PERSONS

NUTRITIONAL VALUE (ESTIMATED AMOUNT PER SERVING)
891 Calories   666 Calories from Fat   74g Total Fat   33g Saturated Fat   0.5g Trans Fat   3.1g Polyunsaturated Fat   30g Monounsaturated Fat   229mg Cholesterol   513mg Sodium   900mg Potassium   1.4g Total Carbohydrates 0.4g Dietary Fiber   0.3g Sugars   52g Protein

INGREDIENTS
- 4 to 5 pound spork loin
- Mango Chipotle Seasoning
- Olive oil
- 1 wooden kabob skewer

DIRECTIONS
1. Rinse the pork loin and then, pat them dry using paper towels.
2. To braid; make two cuts lengthwise on the loin (you should have be having three connected strands). Cut the loin lengthwise & all the way through.
3. Pour and rub a small quantity of olive oil over the loin then, coat the meat with the pork rubs, any of your favorite.
4. Next, braid the pork pieces together and then, take a wooden skewer; stick through the ends of pieces.
5. Preheat the grill of your wood pellets over Hi Smoke for a couple of minutes. Place the coated loin over the grill & cook for an hour. Once done; turn the heat to 275 F & continue to cook until the internal temperature of the meat reflects 145 F. Pull off the grill and then, wrap in aluminum foil; let the loin to rest for 12 to 15 minutes. Slice & enjoy.

Smoked Mustard & Brown Sugar Ham

PREP TIME: 20 MINUTES

COOKING TIME: 4 HOURS & 20 MINUTES
SERVINGS: 12 PERSONS

NUTRITIONAL VALUE (ESTIMATED AMOUNT PER SERVING)
890 Calories   343 Calories from Fat   38g Total Fat   12g Saturated Fat   0g Trans Fat   4.2g Polyunsaturated Fat   18g Monounsaturated Fat   240mg Cholesterol   5819mg Sodium   1425mg Potassium   50g Total Carbohydrates 0.1g Dietary Fiber   39g Sugars   83g Protein

INGREDIENTS
- 12 to 15 pound cured ham
- Pineapple juice for basting
- 1 pound brown sugar
- Fruit or apple hardwood pellets
- 1 bottle Dijon mustard

DIRECTIONS

1. Preheat your pellet smoker or pellet grill over 225 F in advance. Unwrap the ham & get rid of any excess moisture using paper towel.

2. Coat the ham with Dijon mustard then, dust the ham lightly with the brown sugar. Place the coated ham in the pellet smoker / grill & smoke for two hours.

3. Once done, remove the ham from pellet grill & place it over aluminum foil sheet. Baste the ham with some pineapple juice. Once you have basted the ham; wrap it in the aluminum foil & place it over the pellet grill again; continue to cook at 225 F for an hour more.

4. Once done, glaze the ham. Unwrap the top of ham; ensure that you let it sitting in the aluminum foil. Once done, heavily sprinkle the meat with brown sugar & baste with the pineapple juice. Place the ham back over the pellet smoker or grill again and cook at 225 F until the internal temperature of the meat reflects 145 F, for 1 hour; let the juice and sugar to prepare your glaze.

5. Remove the ham from pellet smoker or grill & loosely tent it with aluminum foil; let it rest for a couple of minutes. Serve hot and enjoy.

Chapter 3: Lamb Recipes

Greek Style Roast Leg Of Lamb

PREP TIME: 25 MINUTES

COOKING TIME: 1 HOUR & 35 MINUTES

SERVINGS: 12 PERSONS

NUTRITIONAL VALUE (ESTIMATED AMOUNT PER SERVING)
769 Calories   575 Calories from Fat   64g Total Fat   26g Saturated Fat   0g Trans Fat   5.2g Polyunsaturated Fat   28g Monounsaturated Fat   191mg Cholesterol   154mg Sodium   618mg Potassium   0.7g Total Carbohydrates 0.1g Dietary Fiber   0g Sugars   45g Protein

INGREDIENTS
- 6 tablespoons extra-virgin olive oil
- 1 Leg of lamb (6 to 7 pounds), bone-in
- Juice of 2 lemons, freshly squeezed
- 2 sprigs of fresh rosemary, stems discarded, stripped needles
- 1 sprig of fresh oregano, or 1 teaspoon Dried
- 8 garlic cloves
- Freshly ground black pepper & kosher salt (coarse) as required

DIRECTIONS
1. Make a chain of small slits in the meat using a sharp paring knife.
2. For herb & garlic paste: Finely mince the rosemary with oregano, and garlic using a chef's knife on a clean, large cutting board. Alternatively, add these ingredients in a food processor.

3. Stuff some of the prepared paste into each of the slits on meat; ensure that you add it into the slit using any of the utensils. Next, add the coated lamb on a rack, preferably inside a large roasting pan. For easier clean-up; don't forget to line the pan with aluminum foil.

4. Rub the outside of meat first with the freshly squeezed lemon juice and then with the olive oil. Using a plastic wrap; cover & refrigerate for overnight.

5. The next day; remove the meat from refrigerator & let sit at room temperature for half an hour.

6. Get rid of the plastic wrap & season the meat with pepper and salt to taste. When ready, preheat the grill of wood pellet on Smoke for 4 to 5 minutes, with the lid open. Set the cooking temperature to 400 F and close the lid.

7. Roast the lamb for half an hour. Decrease the heat to 350 F & continue cooking for an hour more, until the internal temperature of the meat reflects 140 F.

8. Transfer the cooked lamb to a large, clean cutting board & let rest for a couple of minutes then, slice diagonally into thin slices. Serve while still hot and enjoy.

Rosemary Lamb

PREP TIME: 20 MINUTES

COOKING TIME: 3 HOURS & 10 MINUTES
SERVINGS: 2 PERSONS

NUTRITIONAL VALUE (ESTIMATED AMOUNT PER SERVING)
668 Calories   516 Calories from Fat   57g Total Fat   27g Saturated Fat   0.9g
Trans Fat   3.6g Polyunsaturated Fat   22g Monounsaturated Fat   150mg
Cholesterol   256mg Sodium   665mg Potassium   17g Total Carbohydrates
2.3g Dietary Fiber   0.8g Sugars   22g Protein

INGREDIENTS
- 1 rack lamb, rib
- A bunch of fresh asparagus
- 2 rosemary, springs
- 1 dozen baby potato
- 2 tablespoons olive oil
- Pepper & salt to taste
- ½ cup butter

DIRECTIONS
1. Preheat the grill of your wood pellet to 225 F in advance.
2. Get rid of the membrane from the back side of the ribs and then, drizzle on both sides with olive oil; finally sprinkle with the rosemary.
3. Combine the butter with potatoes in a deep baking dish.
4. Place the rack of prepared ribs alongside the dish of potatoes on the grates. Smoke until the internal temperature of the meat reflects 145 F, for 3 hours. During the last 15 minutes of cooking don't forget to add asparagus to the potatoes & continue to cook until turn tender.
5. Slice the lamb into desired pieces & serve with cooked asparagus and potatoes.

Smoked Rack Of Lamb

PREP TIME: 20 MINUTES

COOKING TIME: 1 HOUR & 20 MINUTES

SERVINGS: 4 PERSONS

NUTRITIONAL VALUE (ESTIMATED AMOUNT PER SERVING)
788 Calories   554 Calories from Fat   62g Total Fat   27g Saturated Fat   0g Trans Fat   4.9g Polyunsaturated Fat   25g Monounsaturated Fat   204mg Cholesterol   630mg Sodium   755mg Potassium   4.5g Total Carbohydrates 0.7g Dietary Fiber   2g Sugars   49g Protein

INGREDIENTS
- A rack of lamb, preferably 4 to 5 pounds

FOR MARINADE
- 1 medium lemon
- 4 garlic cloves, minced
- 1 teaspoon thyme
- ¼ cup balsamic vinegar
- 1 teaspoon basil
- 1 teaspoon each of pepper & salt

FOR GLAZE
- 2 tablespoons soy sauce
- ¼ cup Dijon mustard
- 2 tablespoons Worcestershire sauce
- ¼ cup dry red wine

DIRECTIONS

1. Combine the entire marinade ingredients together in a gallon-sized zip lock bag. Once done, trim the silver skin from the lamb racks and then, add the trimmed racks into the gallon bag with the marinade; mix the pieces well & refrigerate for overnight.

2. The next day, preheat your wood pellet to 300 F in advance. In the meantime, combine the entire glaze ingredients together in a large-sized mixing bowl.

3. Once the glaze is mixed and the grill is preheated, place the rack of lamb over the hot grill. Cook the racks for 12 to 15 minutes and then, baste with the prepared glaze mixture; flip & cook the meat until the internal temperature reflects somewhere between 135 to 145 F, approximately for an hour; don't forget to baste the meat with the glaze after every half an hour. Once done, remove the meat from grill & let sit for a couple of minutes. Once done, cut the meat into desired pieces; serve hot & enjoy.

Smoked Lamb Chops (Lollipops)

PREP TIME: 20 MINUTES

COOKING TIME: 55 MINUTES

SERVINGS: 4 PERSONS

NUTRITIONAL VALUE (ESTIMATED AMOUNT PER SERVING)
184 Calories   148 Calories from Fat   16g Total Fat   3.3g Saturated Fat   0.2g
Trans Fat   1.6g Polyunsaturated Fat   11g Monounsaturated Fat   12mg
Cholesterol   12mg ill Sodium   75mg Potassium   6g Total Carbohydrates
0.4g Dietary Fiber   4.7g Sugars   4.2g Protein

INGREDIENTS
- 2 tablespoons fresh sage
- 1 rack of lamb
- 2 garlic cloves, large, roughly chopped
- 1 tablespoon fresh thyme
- 3 sprigs of fresh rosemary, approximately 2 tablespoons
- ¼ cup olive oil
- 2 tablespoons shallots, roughly chopped
- 1 tablespoon honey
- ½ teaspoon each of course ground pepper & salt

DIRECTIONS
1. Using a fruit wood; preheat your smoker to 225 F in advance.
2. Trim any silver skin & excess fat from the rack of lamb.
3. Thoroughly combine the leftover ingredients together (for the herb paste) in a food processor & liberally apply the paste over the rack of lamb.
4. Place the coated lamb on the preheated smoker & cook until the internal temperature of the rack of lamb reflects 120 F, for 45 minutes to 55 minutes. Remove the meat & prepare your smoker or grill for direct heat now.
5. Sear the lamb for a couple of minutes on each side. Let rest for 5 minutes and then, slice into individual lollipops; serve hot & enjoy.

Smoked Loin Lamb Chops

PREP TIME: 20 MINUTES

COOKING TIME: 1 HOUR & 20 MINUTES

SERVINGS: 6 PERSONS

NUTRITIONAL VALUE (ESTIMATED AMOUNT PER SERVING)
652 Calories   476 Calories from Fat   53g Total Fat   21g Saturated Fat   0g
Trans Fat   2.3g Polyunsaturated Fat   23g Monounsaturated Fat   159mg
Cholesterol   111mg Sodium   693mg Potassium   0.2g Total Carbohydrates
0.1g Dietary Fiber   0g Sugars   41g Protein

INGREDIENTS
- 10 to 12 Lamb loin chops
- Jeff's Original rub recipe
- Rosemary , finely chopped
- Olive oil
- Coarse kosher salt

DIRECTIONS
1. Place the chops on a cookie sheet or cooling rack.
2. To dry brine, generously sprinkle the top of chops with salt.
3. Place in a fridge for an hour or two.
4. Once done; remove the coated meat from fridge; ensure that you don't rinse the meat.
5. Prepare an infusion of olive oil and rosemary by pouring approximately ¼ cup of the olive oil on top of 1 tablespoon of the chopped rosemary; set the mixture aside and let sit for an hour.
6. Brush the prepared mixture on top & sides of your lamb chops.
7. Generously sprinkle the top, sides and bottom of chops with the rub.
8. Preheat your smoker at 225 F on indirect heat.

9. For great results, ensure that you use a mixture of apple and pecan for smoke.
10. Cook the coated chops for 40 to 50 minutes, until the internal temperature of chops reflects 138 F.
11. Let rest on the counter for 5 to 7 minutes, with foil tented.
12. Serve hot and enjoy.

Chapter 4: Chicken Recipes

Chesapeake Garlic Parmesan Wings

PREP TIME: 15 MINUTES

COOKING TIME: 1 HOUR & 35 MINUTES

SERVINGS: 6 PERSONS

NUTRITIONAL VALUE (ESTIMATED AMOUNT PER SERVING)
1035 Calories   712 Calories from Fat   79g Total Fat   35g Saturated Fat   1.5g Trans Fat   11g Polyunsaturated Fat   27g Monounsaturated Fat   249mg Cholesterol   2785mg Sodium   513mg Potassium   43g Total Carbohydrates   1.3g Dietary Fiber   19g Sugars   40g Protein

INGREDIENTS

FOR WINGS
- 2 to 4 pounds chicken wings
- Pepper & salt to taste

FOR GARLIC PARMESAN SAUCE
- 1 cup hot sauce, any of your favorite
- 2 tablespoons parmesan, grated
- 1 stick of butter
- 2 tablespoons minced garlic
- 1 teaspoon old bay seasoning
- ¼ cup raw honey

DIRECTIONS

1. Preheat your pellet grill at 350 F in advance.
2. Cook the chicken wings until an internal temperature reflects 145 F.
3. In the meantime, prepare the sauce. Next, over moderate heat in a large sauce pan; heat the entire sauce ingredients together. Slowly add the butter & give the ingredients a good stir until the butter is melted completely. Continue to stir the ingredient until the sauce ingredients and butter are mixed evenly; set the mixture aside.
4. Prepare a Dutch oven with oil for frying. Heat the oil until very hot.
5. Remove the chicken pieces from smoker & put the chicken into the fry basket. Fry the chicken for a couple of minutes, until they reflect internal temperature of 165 F.
6. Place the cooked wings on a baking sheet lined with paper towel & continue to cook for 5 to 10 more minutes.
7. Toss the wings with prepared sauce until covered completely. Serve hot and enjoy.

Pineapple Habanero Wings

PREP TIME: 20 MINUTES

COOKING TIME: 55 MINUTES

SERVINGS: 6 PERSONS

NUTRITIONAL VALUE (ESTIMATED AMOUNT PER SERVING)
919 Calories   549 Calories from Fat   61g Total Fat   23g Saturated Fat   0.8g Trans Fat   10g Polyunsaturated Fat   22g Monounsaturated Fat   201mg Cholesterol   946mg Sodium   560mg Potassium   53g Total Carbohydrates 1.9g Dietary Fiber   27g Sugars   39g Protein

INGREDIENTS

FOR WINGS
- 2-4 pounds chicken wings
- Juice of 2 limes, freshly squeezed
- Jamaican flavored rub

FOR THE PINEAPPLE HABANERO SAUCE
- ½ cup brown sugar
- 3 garlic cloves, minced
- 1 pineapple, cut into spears & grilled until grill marks appear
- ½ yellow pepper, diced
- 1 habanero, seeded & diced
- 1/3 cup white vinegar
- 2 tablespoons softened butter
- Salt to taste

DIRECTIONS

FOR WINGS

1. Drizzle the lime juice over the chicken wings; ensure that they are nicely covered & then, generously season them with the Jamaican rub; set aside and let them marinate for overnight.

FOR HABANERO SAUCE

1. Blend the entire ingredients together in a food processor or blender (don't add the butter). Pour the prepared mixture into a sauce pan with the softened butter & let simmer on medium heat for 10 to 15 minutes.
2. Preheat your pellet smoker in advance to 225 F.
3. Smoke the wings for 40 to 45 minutes; carefully flip & increase the temperature to 350 F.
4. Cook them until they reflect an internal temperature of somewhere 175 to 180 F.
5. Remove the pieces from pellet grill & apply the prepared sauce on each wing.
6. Increase your pellet grill's temperature to 450 F and put the pieces on the grill again; cook until the sauce is set, for 5 to 7 more minutes. Serve hot and enjoy.

Apricot Chipotle Chicken Thighs

PREP TIME: 20 MINUTES

COOKING TIME: 1 HOUR & 20 MINUTES

SERVINGS: 8 PERSONS

NUTRITIONAL VALUE (ESTIMATED AMOUNT PER SERVING)
574 Calories   302 Calories from Fat   34g Total Fat   9.1g Saturated Fat   0.2g Trans Fat   7.3g Polyunsaturated Fat   14g Monounsaturated Fat   216mg Cholesterol   660mg Sodium   525mg Potassium   32g Total Carbohydrates   0.6g Dietary Fiber   22g Sugars   38g Protein

INGREDIENTS
- 3 to 4 pounds bone-in chicken thighs
- 1 teaspoon smoked paprika
- Apricot preserves, preferably 12 ounce
- ¼ cup BBQ sauce
- 1 teaspoon garlic powder
- 2-3 tablespoons chipotle peppers (diced) in adobo sauce
- ¼ cup chicken broth
- 1 tablespoon chipotle seasoning
- 2 tablespoons Dijon mustard
- ¼ teaspoon salt

DIRECTIONS
1. Add the apricot preserves followed by garlic powder, smoked paprika, dijon mustard, chicken broth, BBQ sauce, mango chipotle seasoning, chipotle peppers and salt in a medium-sized mixing bowl; give the ingredients a good stir for a couple of minutes, until combined well. Set approximately ½ cup aside for later use.

2. Place the chicken thighs into a freezer bag; add the prepared apricot chipotle marinade; seal the bag & cover the chicken pieces evenly with the prepared marinade.
3. Let marinade for a couple of hours.
4. Preheat your pellet grill to 400 F in advance.
5. Carefully place the coated chicken pieces over the hot grill, skin side down first & grill until the grill marks start to appear, for 10 minutes. Flip the chicken pieces & continue to grill until an internal temperature reflects 165 F.
6. Remove the pieces from grill & brush them with the kept-aside glaze mixture. Serve hot & enjoy.

Chapter 5: Turkey Recipes

Smoked Turkey

PREP TIME: 20 MINUTES

COOKING TIME: 1 HOUR & 55 MINUTES

SERVINGS: 10 PERSONS

NUTRITIONAL VALUE (ESTIMATED AMOUNT PER SERVING)
873 Calories   359 Calories from Fat   40g Total Fat   14g Saturated Fat   0.7g Trans Fat   8.3g Polyunsaturated Fat   12g Monounsaturated Fat   416mg Cholesterol   1990mg Sodium   1253mg Potassium   2.2g Total Carbohydrates   0.4g Dietary Fiber   0.6g Sugars   50g Protein

INGREDIENTS
- 1 whole turkey
- ½ lemon, medium-sized
- Poultry rub, any of your favorite to coat
- 1 stick of softened butter, at room temperature
- ½ cup of white wine, chicken broth or liquid of choice
- 2 tablespoons each of pepper & salt

DIRECTIONS
1. Preheat your pellet grill over high smoke in advance.
2. Remove the neck and giblets from the turkey then, rinse under water; pat it dry using paper towels.
3. Next, combine the butter with pepper and salt in a small-sized mixing bowl.

4. Gently separate the skin from legs and breast using your hands (ensure that you keep it attached & in a single piece).
5. Pour & evenly spread the prepared butter mixture underneath the skin. Season the turkey with the poultry seasoning (on the outer part).
6. Fill the Turkey Cannon Infusion Roaster with approximately lemon & ½ cup of liquid. Next, smoke the turkey on high smoke for an hour. Set the temperature of your pellet grill to 350 F & continue to cook the turkey until the internal temperature of the meat reflects 160 F. Set aside & let rest roughly for half an hour. Serve and enjoy.

Spatchcock Turkey

PREP TIME: 20 MINUTES

COOKING TIME: 1 HOUR & 20 MINUTES

SERVINGS: 12 PERSONS

NUTRITIONAL VALUE (ESTIMATED AMOUNT PER SERVING)
837 Calories   290 Calories from Fat   32g Total Fat   8.4g Saturated Fat   0.3g Trans Fat   8.4g Polyunsaturated Fat   10g Monounsaturated Fat   413mg Cholesterol   686mg Sodium   1417mg Potassium   4.8g Total Carbohydrates 1.1g Dietary Fiber   2.3g Sugars   125g Protein

INGREDIENTS

FOR THE TURKEY
- 1 whole turkey (roughly 15 pounds), thawed
- Salt to taste

FOR TURKEY STOCK INGREDIENTS
- 4 carrots, sliced
- 1 onion, chopped
- 5 springs fresh thyme
- 1 quart unsalted chicken stock
- 5 springs fresh sage
- 1 quart water
- 4 stalks of celery, chopped

DIRECTIONS
1. Remove the giblet packet and neck from inside the turkey; set aside.
2. Cut out the back bone using kitchen shears or a sharp knife & set aside.
3. Lay the turkey flat, on a metal rack & generously apply the dry brine on both sides (salt). Place in a refrigerator for overnight to air dry.

4. Next, put the entire ingredients for turkey stock in a large-sized roasting pan. Place the roasting pan over the pellet grill & put the top shelf in its place (placing the turkey over the top shelf).
5. Grill the turkey until the internal temperature reflects 160 F, at 350 F.
6. Strain the turkey stock & feel free to use it in gravy. Serve hot and enjoy.

Tequila Lime Roasted Turkey

PREP TIME: 25 MINUTES

COOKING TIME: 2 HOURS & 35 MINUTES

SERVINGS: 12 PERSONS

NUTRITIONAL VALUE (ESTIMATED AMOUNT PER SERVING)
517 Calories   341 Calories from Fat   38g Total Fat   17g Saturated Fat   1.8g Polyunsaturated Fat   18g Monounsaturated Fat   154mg Cholesterol   118mg Sodium   558mg Potassium   0.3g Total Carbohydrates   0g Dietary Fiber   0g Sugars   44g Protein

INGREDIENTS
- 9 garlic cloves
- 1 bone-in whole turkey (roughly 15 pounds), thawed
- 3 jalapeño chiles, cut in half & seeded
- 1 ¼ cups gold tequila
- 3 ounces olive oil
- 1 ½ teaspoons pepper
- 3 limes, cut into wedges
- 1 ¼ cups lime juice, fresh
- ¾ cups each of orange juice & chicken broth
- 3 tablespoon chili powder
- 1 tablespoon salt

DIRECTIONS
1. Preheat your smoker to 325 F in advance. Place the turkey breast in a shallow roasting pan, preferably skin side up.
2. Place the jalapeno & garlic in a mini food processor. Cover & process on high power until chopped finely. Add the chili powder followed by 3 ounces of

tequila, 3 ounces of lime juice, oil, pepper and salt. Cover & process on high power again until the mixture is completely smooth.

3. Next, using spoon or fingers; loosen the turkey skin & rub the prepared garlic mixture over and under the turkey skin; evenly pour the leftover mix on top of the turkey. Insert an ovenproof meat thermometer into the thickest part of the breast & ensure that it doesn't touch the bone.

4. Pour the broth and orange juice followed by the leftover lime juice and tequila into a roasting pan.

5. Roast until the thermometer reflects a reading of 165 F, uncovered. Place the turkey on a warm platter and then, cover with aluminum foil. Let stand for 12 to 15 minutes before carving. Spoon the pan juices on top of the turkey & garnish your dish with some fresh lime wedges. Enjoy.

Chapter 6: Fish Recipes

Japanese Smoked Salmon

PREP TIME: 20 MINUTES

COOKING TIME: 1 HOUR & 10 MINUTES

SERVINGS: 6 PERSONS

NUTRITIONAL VALUE (ESTIMATED AMOUNT PER SERVING)
180 Calories   149 Calories from Fat   17g Total Fat   2.6g Saturated Fat   0g Trans Fat   2.7g Polyunsaturated Fat   10g Monounsaturated Fat   16mg Cholesterol   788mg Sodium   172mg Potassium   1.1g Total Carbohydrates   0.2g Dietary Fiber   0.1g Sugars   7g Protein

INGREDIENTS
- 2 salmon, fillets (skin removed)
- 1 teaspoon black pepper
- 3 cedar plank, untreated
- 1 teaspoon garlic, minced
- 1/3 cup soy sauce
- 1 teaspoon fresh parsley, minced
- 1/3 cup olive oil
- 1 teaspoon sesame oil
- 1 ½ tablespoons rice vinegar
- 1 teaspoon onion, salt

DIRECTIONS

1. For Japanese Salmon Marinade: Combine olive oil with sesame oil, rice vinegar, minced garlic, and soy sauce in a large-sized mixing bowl until evenly mixed. Add the salmon fillets; turning the pieces several times until nice coated & let marinate for an hour, at room temperature.

2. Soak the cedar planks for an hour or two in warm water.

3. Preheat your grill on smoke with the lid open for a couple of minutes, until you could see a fire in the burn pot. Preheat it to 225 F in advance. Once done; place the cedar planks on the grate and wait until the boards crackle a little & start to smoke.

4. Remove the fish from marinade and then, generously season it with the parsley, onion powder & black pepper; discard any excess marinade. Carefully place the coated salmon over the planks & grill for 25 to 30 minutes, until the internal temperature reads 140 F.

5. Remove from the grill & let rest for a couple of minutes; serve hot & enjoy.

Grilled Salmon

PREP TIME: 20 MINUTES

COOKING TIME: 20 MINUTES

SERVINGS: 4 PERSONS

NUTRITIONAL VALUE (ESTIMATED AMOUNT PER SERVING)
211 Calories   133 Calories from Fat   15g Total Fat   3.1g Saturated Fat   0g
Trans Fat   3.7g Polyunsaturated Fat   5.7g Monounsaturated Fat   47mg
Cholesterol   196mg Sodium   331mg Potassium   1.3g Total Carbohydrates
0.4g Dietary Fiber   0.3g Sugars   18g Protein

INGREDIENTS
- 4 (6 to 8 ounces) salmon fillets (with skin), remove the pin bones
- Extra-virgin olive oil
- ½ lemon, cut into 4 wedges
- Freshly ground black pepper & kosher salt to taste

DIRECTIONS
1. Preheat your grill over medium-high heat (approximately 400 to 450 F), for direct cooking. When the grill is nearly 350 F, place the cast-iron skillet or griddle in the middle of your grill & let it get hot as well.
2. Pat dry the salmon using paper towels and then, generously brush the pieces with oil & then, season with pepper and salt, preferably the flesh side.
3. Carefully, place the coated fillets directly over the hot griddle using a metal spatula, flesh side down first. It's important for you to evenly space the fillets. Close the lid & let the fillets to sear for a couple of minutes, until they don't stick and you can easily lift them off the griddle, over direct medium-high heat.
4. Carefully turn over the fillets; close the lid & continue cooking for 3 to 5 more minutes, until you get your desired doneness. Slip a spatula between the flesh and skin then, transfer the cooked fillets to warmed, individual serving plates. Serve immediately with some fresh lemon wedges on side and enjoy.

Grilled Fresh Fish

PREP TIME: 10 MINUTES

COOKING TIME: 25 MINUTES

SERVINGS: 4 PERSONS

NUTRITIONAL VALUE (ESTIMATED AMOUNT PER SERVING)
30 Calories   2.5 Calories from Fat   0.3g Total Fat   0.1g Saturated Fat   0g Trans Fat   0.1g Polyunsaturated Fat   0g Monounsaturated Fat   16mg Cholesterol   20mg Sodium   146mg Potassium   3.9g Total Carbohydrates   1.2g Dietary Fiber   1.1g Sugars   4.4g Protein

INGREDIENTS
- 1 whole firm white fish fillet: such as halibut, sea bass or cod
- 2 whole lemons; sliced into half
- Traeger Fin & Feather Rub, as required

DIRECTIONS
1. Preheat your wood pellet to 325 F in advance for 12 to 15 minutes, lid closed.
2. Season the fish with Rub & let sit for half an hour.
3. Place the fish & lemons directly over the hot grill grates, cut side down. Cook until the fish is flaky, for 12 to 15 minutes. Ensure that you don't overcook the fish. Serve immediately with grilled lemons and enjoy.

Chapter 7: Seafood Recipes

Grilled Texas Spicy Shrimp

PREP TIME: 20 MINUTES

COOKING TIME: 20 MINUTES

SERVINGS: 8 PERSONS

NUTRITIONAL VALUE (ESTIMATED AMOUNT PER SERVING)
162 Calories   28 Calories from Fat   3.1g Total Fat   0.6g Saturated Fat   0g Trans Fat   0.6g Polyunsaturated Fat   1.5g Monounsaturated Fat   143mg Cholesterol   1006mg Sodium   235mg Potassium   17g Total Carbohydrates   0.6g Dietary Fiber   12g Sugars 16g Protein

INGREDIENTS
- 2 pounds jumbo shrimp, peeled & deveined; washed; drain & pat dry
- 1 whole jalapeño pepper, seeded and minced
- 2 garlic clove, minced
- ½ cup fresh cilantro, finely chopped
- 1 small onion, finely diced
- 3 plus 1 tablespoons olive oil
- 1 cup BBQ Sauce
- Ground black pepper & salt to taste

DIRECTIONS
1. Transfer the clean shrimp to a large-sized mixing bowl.
2. Gently mix with 2 tablespoons of oil and then, generously season with pepper and salt to taste; set aside until ready to use.

3. For Sauce: Over medium-low heat in a large saucepan; heat 1 tablespoon of olive oil until hot. Once done; add the jalapeño pepper, onion and garlic; sauté for a couple of minutes, until turn softened and then, stir in the barbecue sauce.

4. When you are ready to cook the shrimp, preheat your wood pellet to 450 F, closed lid.

5. Carefully arrange the shrimp pieces over the hot grill grate & cook until the shrimp is firm, opaque & cooked through, for 2 to 3 minutes on each side.

6. Quickly transfer the cooked shrimp along with the freshly chopped cilantro into the warm sauce. Gently stir the ingredients until nicely coated; serve & enjoy.

Bacon Wrapped Scallops

PREP TIME: 20 MINUTES

COOKING TIME: 20 MINUTES

SERVINGS: 8 PERSONS

NUTRITIONAL VALUE (ESTIMATED AMOUNT PER SERVING)
157 Calories   104 Calories from Fat   12g Total Fat   3.8g Saturated Fat   0g
Trans Fat   1.9g Polyunsaturated Fat   5g Monounsaturated Fat   32mg
Cholesterol   483mg Sodium   172mg Potassium   2.2g Total Carbohydrates
0g Dietary Fiber   0.3g Sugars   10g Protein

INGREDIENTS
- ½ pound bacon
- 1 pound sea scallops, large; dry using paper towels
- Sea salt to taste

DIRECTIONS
1. Preheat your pellet grill per the instructions to 350 F in advance.
2. Wrap the scallops in a cut piece of bacon & secure each piece using a toothpick.
3. Lay the scallops over the hot grill, bacon-side-down. Close the lid & cook for 5 to 7 minutes then, carefully rotate the pieces. Continue to cook evenly cooked on all sides. Serve hot & enjoy.

Veracruz Scallops with Green Chile Sauce

PREP TIME: 20 MINUTES

COOKING TIME: 20 MINUTES

SERVINGS: 8 PERSONS

NUTRITIONAL VALUE (ESTIMATED AMOUNT PER SERVING)
208 Calories   182 Calories from Fat   20g Total Fat   4.3g Saturated Fat   0.3g Trans Fat   10g Polyunsaturated Fat   4.6g Monounsaturated Fat   22mg Cholesterol   698mg Sodium   168mg Potassium   5g Total Carbohydrates   0.9g Dietary Fiber   2.3g Sugars   2.4g Protein

INGREDIENTS
- 24 (2 ounces) sea scallops, large pieces
- Finely grated juice and zest of 1 lime, fresh
- Vegetable oil, as required

FOR RUB
- 1 teaspoon pure chile powder
- ½ teaspoon ground cumin
- 1 teaspoon paprika
- ½ teaspoon oregano, dried
- 1 teaspoon kosher salt
- ¼ teaspoon freshly ground black pepper

FOR SAUCE
- 3 long Anaheim chile peppers
- ½ cup sour cream
- 3 scallions (green and white parts only), coarsely chopped
- ½ cup mayonnaise

- 1 garlic clove, small
- ¼ cup fresh cilantro leaves & tender stems; loosely packed
- Finely grated juice & zest of 1 lime, fresh
- ¼ teaspoon kosher salt

DIRECTIONS

1. Preheat the grill over high heat for direct cooking
2. Grill the chile peppers for a couple of minutes, until turn blackened & blistered in spots, with the lid open, turning every now and then. Remove the chiles from grill; set aside until easy to handle. Once done; remove the stem ends & discard. Scrape off & discard the blackened skins using a sharp knife. Coarsely chop the leftover parts of chiles & drop them into a blender or food processor. Add the scallions followed by garlic, and cilantro. Process on high power until you get coarse paste like consistency; scraping down the sides of your bowl as required. Add the leftover sauce ingredients & process on high power again until you get smooth sauce.
3. Next, mix the entire rub ingredients together in a small-sized mixing bowl.
4. Rinse the scallops under cold running tap water & remove the tough, small muscle. Place the cleaned scallops in a large-sized mixing bowl & add oil (enough to coat). Add the rub mixture followed by the lime juice, and lime zest. Mix well until the scallops are evenly coated.
5. Grill the scallops for 4 to 6 minutes, until opaque in the middle and firm slightly on the surface, with the lid closed, turning once. Remove from the grill; serve warm with the prepared sauce and enjoy.

Chapter 8: Vegetables Recipes

Herb Roasted Potatoes

PREP TIME: 20 MINUTES

COOKING TIME: 1 HOUR & 20 MINUTES

SERVINGS: 8 PERSONS

NUTRITIONAL VALUE (ESTIMATED AMOUNT PER SERVING)
224 Calories   48 Calories from Fat   5.3g Total Fat   0.8g Saturated Fat   0g Trans Fat   0.6g Polyunsaturated Fat   3.7g Monounsaturated Fat   0mg Cholesterol   14mg Sodium   981mg Potassium   41g Total Carbohydrates   5g Dietary Fiber   1.9g Sugars   4.9g Protein

INGREDIENTS
- 4 pounds yellow potatoes, cubed into small, pieces; preferably bite-sized
- 2 tablespoons fresh rosemary, chopped
- 6 garlic cloves, minced
- 2 tablespoons fresh thyme, chopped
- 3 tablespoons olive oil
- 2 tablespoons fresh sage, chopped
- Salt and pepper to taste

DIRECTIONS
1. Preheat your pellet grill to 375 F in advance.
2. Cube the potatoes & mix them with garlic, oil and herbs. Spread a thin layer of coated potatoes in a skillet (preferably cast iron) & roast for an hour, until turn golden brown, soft & crispy. Stirring the potatoes once during the roasting process; serve hot & enjoy.

Grilled Corn on the Cob

PREP TIME: 20 MINUTES

COOKING TIME: 30 MINUTES

SERVINGS: 2 PERSONS

NUTRITIONAL VALUE (ESTIMATED AMOUNT PER SERVING)
90 Calories   6.3 Calories from Fat   0.7g Total Fat   0.2g Saturated Fat   0g Trans Fat   0.2g Polyunsaturated Fat   0.1g Monounsaturated Fat   0.9mg Cholesterol   52mg Sodium   291mg Potassium   19g Total Carbohydrates   3.2g Dietary Fiber   2.3g Sugars   3.6g Protein

INGREDIENTS
- Corn on the cob, fresh
- Butter & salt for serving

DIRECTIONS
1. Preheat your pellet grill over high heat in advance.
2. Remove a few outer layers of the corn husks.
3. Remove the top from each cob using scissors & trim any loose husk leaves as well. Place the corn over the hot grill (preferably in their husks) & close the lid. Cook for 25 to 30 minutes, until all sides of the husks turn charred, turning after every 8 to 10 minutes.
4. Remove the corn from grill. Let sit until you can easily handle it, for a couple of minutes. Remove the charred husks & silks from the corn.
5. Apply some butter and salt on hot corn; rubbing it nicely. Serve hot and enjoy.

Smoked Mashed Potatoes

PREP TIME: 20 MINUTES

COOKING TIME: 2 HOURS & 20 MINUTES

SERVINGS: 4 PERSONS

NUTRITIONAL VALUE (ESTIMATED AMOUNT PER SERVING)
422 Calories   138 Calories from Fat   15g Total Fat   8.4g Saturated Fat   0.6g Trans Fat   0.7g Polyunsaturated Fat   3.7g Monounsaturated Fat   46mg Cholesterol   320mg Sodium   1419mg Potassium   62g Total Carbohydrates   4.9g Dietary Fiber   12g Sugars   11g Protein

INGREDIENTS
- 6 russet potatoes
- 1 cube butter, melted
- 2 sweet potatoes
- 1 cup sour cream
- 2 tablespoons chives, chopped
- 1 pint buttermilk
- Garlic salt, pepper & salt to taste

DIRECTIONS
1. Preheat your pellet grill over Hi Smoke in advance. When done, place the entire potatoes over the hot grate.
2. Smoke the potatoes until turn fork tender, for 2 hours. Next, using a hand mixer or fork; mash the potatoes. Add the butter followed by buttermilk, chives, sour cream, garlic salt, pepper, and salt; mix well. Serve hot & enjoy.

Chapter 9: Smoking Tips

TYPES OF SMOKERS

ELECTRIC SMOKERS

The electric smoker is the best smoker because it is very simple to use. Just set it, put your food in it and leave the rest of the work to the smoker. There is nothing an electric smoker can't grill, be it seafood, poultry, meat, cheese or bread. It requires little attention unlike other smokers like filling water bin, lighting wood or charcoal and checking on fuel frequently. Yes, unlike traditional smoker, electric smoker just need 2 to 4 ounce of wood chips that turns out a delicious and flavorful smoky food. Furthermore, they maintain cooking temperature really well. On the other hand, it sleek and stylish look and small size make it appropriate if you are living in an apartment or condo. Due to their simpler functions and hassle-free cooking, the electric smoker is a good choice for beginner cooks who want to get started with smoking food.

GAS SMOKERS

Gas smokers or propane smoker are much like a gas grill using propane as a fuel. Therefore, the heat for cooking remains consistent and steady. Furthermore, gas smokers are as easy to use, just set the temperature and walk away. However, frequent checks need to be done to make sure fuel doesn't run out. It isn't a big issue but one should keep in mind. And the best part, a gas smoker can be used when there is no electricity or when you need an oven. A gas smoker can take up to cooking temperature to 450 degrees, making this smoker flexible to be used as an oven. Another fantastic feature of gas smoker is its portability so they can use anywhere. Just pack it and take it along with you on your camping trips or other outdoor adventures.

CHARCOAL SMOKERS

Nothing can beat the flavor charcoal gives to your food. Its best flavor just simply can't match with any other smoker flavor. Unfortunately, setting a charcoal smoker, tuning fuel, maintaining cooking temperature and checking food can be a pain and you might burn the food. Not to worry, these hassles of a charcoal smoker does go away with practice and experience. Therefore, a charcoal smoker suits perfectly for serious grillers and barbecue purist who want flavors.

PELLET SMOKERS

Pellet smokers are making a surge due to their best feature of a pallet of maintaining a consistent temperature. It contains an automated system to drop pallets which frees the cook to monitor fuel level. The addition of thermostat gives the user the complete control the cooking temperature and grilling of food under ideal condition. In addition, the smoking food uses the heat from hardwood which gives food a delicious flavor. The only downside of pallet smoker is their high cost between the ranges of $100 to %600.

TYPES OF SMOKER WOODS

Smoker wood is an important element which you need to decide correctly to cook a delicious smoked food. The reason is that smoker chips of woods impart different flavors on the food you are cooking in the smoker. Therefore, you should know which smoker wood should be used to create a delicious smoked food. Here is the lowdown of smoker woods and which food is best with them.

1. 1- Alder: A lighter smoker wood with natural sweetness.
2. Best to smoke: Any fish especially salmon, poultry and game birds.
3. 2- Maple: This smoker wood has a mild and sweet flavor. In addition, its sweet smoke gives the food a dark appearance. For better flavor, use it as a combination with alder, apple or oak smoker woods.
4. Best to smoke: Vegetables, cheese, and poultry.
5. 3- Apple: A mild fruity flavor smoker wood with natural sweetness. When mixed with oak smoker wood, it gives a great flavor to food. Let food smoke for several hours as the smoke takes a while to permeate the food with the flavors.
6. Best to smoke: Poultry, beef, pork, lamb, and seafood.
7. 4- Cherry: This smoker wood is an all-purpose fruity flavor wood for any type of meat. Its smoke gives the food a rich, mahogany color. Try smoking by mixing it with alder, oak, pecan and hickory smoker wood.
8. Best to smoke: Chicken, turkey, ham, pork, and beef.
9. 5- Oak: Oakwood gives a medium flavor to food which is stronger compared to apple wood and cherry wood and lighter compared to hickory. This versatile smoker wood works well blended with hickory, apple, and cherry woods.
10. Best to smoke: Sausages, brisket, and lamb.
11. 6- Peach and Pear: Both smoker woods are similar to each other. They give food a subtle light and fruity flavor with the addition of natural sweetness.
12. Best to smoke: Poultry, pork and game birds.

13. 7- Hickory: Hickory wood infuses a strong sweet and bacon flavor into the food, especially meat cuts. Don't over smoke with this wood as it can turn the taste of food bitter.
14. Best to smoke: Red meat, poultry, pork shoulder, ribs.
15. 8- Pecan: This sweet smoker wood lends the food a rich and nutty flavor. Use it with Mesquite wood to balance its sweetness.
16. Best to smoke: Poultry, pork.
17. 9- Walnut: This strong flavored smoker wood is often used as a mixing wood due to its slightly bitter flavor. Use walnut wood with lighter smoke woods like pecan wood or apple wood.
18. Best to smoke: Red meat and game birds.
19. 10- Grape: Grape wood chips give a sweet berry flavor to food. It's best to use these wood chips with apple wood chips.
20. Best to smoke: Poultry
21. 11- Mulberry: Mulberry wood chips is similar to apple wood chips. It adds natural sweetness and gives berry finish to the food.
22. Best to smoke: Ham and Chicken.
23. 12- Mesquite: Mesquite wood chips flavor is earthy and slightly harsh and bitter. It burns fast and strongly hot. Therefore, don't use it for longer grilling.
24. Best to smoke: Red meat, dark meat.

THE DIFFERENT TYPES OF CHARCOAL AND THEIR BENEFITS

Charcoal is one of the efficient fuels for smoking. It burns hot, with more concentrated fire. Smoking food with charcoal is awesome. Though lighting charcoals, regulating airflows and controlling the heat is always a challenge, however, the excellent taste of food is worth this challenge. But, keep in mind that not all charcoals are equal and selecting one is a matter of preference.

LUMP CHARCOAL:

Lump charcoal or hardwood is the first choice of griller as a better fuel source. It is basically made by burning wood logs in an underground pit for a few days. As a result, water, sap, and other substances in log burn out, leaving behind a pure char or lump charcoal. This charcoal burns pure, hot and efficiently. They burn hotter in the beginner and burn cooler by the end. Therefore, lump charcoal is a good choice for broiling quickly or searing food at intense heat. In addition, the lump char also add the aroma of wood smoke into the food which takes the taste to another level of gastronomical heaven. Since, lump charcoal cool its fire in 30 minutes, replenish fire to maintain the temperature which takes only 5 to 10 minutes by adding few unlit coals. It's recommended to use lump charcoal with a combination of wood chips like maple, oak or hickory and refuel this wood chips every 40 minutes during smoking food.

CHARCOAL BRIQUETTES:

Charcoal briquettes are actually crushed charcoal. The major benefit of using this natural charcoal is its even shape and size. This is done by adding chemical binders and fillers like coal dust and compressing into a pillow shape. Therefore, creating a bed of coals is very easy with charcoal briquettes which are quite hard with uneven and irregular charcoals. The only downside is that they burn very quickly, more than lump charcoal. This creates a short window for smoking food, therefore, more briquettes need to add during grilling.

THE DIFFERENCE BETWEEN BARBECUING A MEAT AND SMOKING IT?

There are two main ways to cook meat that has become an increasingly popular cooking method: smoking or barbecuing. They are both different and require different cooking equipment, temperature, and timing. Following is the full comparison between smoking and barbecue.

BARBECUING MEAT:

Barbecue is a slow cooking, indirectly over low heat between 200 to 250 degrees F. Therefore, it is best suited for beef brisket, whole pig, turkeys or pork shoulder. These animals tend to have tough muscles which need slow cooking over low heat to get a moist and tender meat. It turns out an extremely tender and flavorful meat. The best example of a perfect barbecue is falling of meat off the bones. During the barbecue, the fuel needs to be filled frequently but do this quickly, as lifting lid of burner exposes meat to air which can turn it dry.

For barbecuing meat, the grill needs to be preheated until hot. For this light enough charcoals or brisquettes so that their fire turns down for cooking. In the meantime, season meat and then when grill reaches to perfect cooking temperature, place seasoned meat on it. Having grill on perfect temperature is essential as meat won't stick to grilling grate.

Equipment: Fire pit, grill or a charcoal burner with lid.

Fueling: Lump wood charcoal, charcoal briquettes or wood chips combination like apple. Cherry and oak wood chips.

Best to smoke: A big cut of meats like Briskets, whole chicken, sausages, jerky, pork, and ribs.

Temperature: 190 to 300 degrees F

Timing: 2 hours to a day long.

SMOKING MEAT:

Smoking is one of the oldest cooking technique dating back to the first people living in caves. It was traditionally a food preservation method and with the time, its popularity never died. Smoking is a related process of barbecue. It's the best cooking method to bring out the rich and deep flavor of meat that tastes heavenly when meat is smoked until it comes off the bone.

During smoking, food is cooked below 200 degrees F cooking temperature. Therefore, smoking food requires a lot of time and patience. It infuses woody flavor into the meat and turns a silky and fall-of-bone meat. There are three ways to smoke food, cold smoke, hot smoke and adding liquid smoke. In these three types of smoking methods, liquid smoke is becoming increasingly common. Its main advantage is that smoke flavor is controlled. In addition, the effect of liquid smoke on meat is immediate.

There is another smoking method which called water smoking. It uses water smoker which is specifically designed to incorporate water in the smoking process. The water helps in controlling the temperature of smoker which is great for large cut meats for long hours.

Equipment: A closed container or high-tech smoker.

Fueling: The container will need an external source for a smoke. Wood chips are burn to add smoky flavor to the meat. However, the frequent check should be made to monitor and adjust temperature for smoking.

Best to smoke: A big cut of meats like Briskets, whole chicken, pork, and ribs.

Temperature: 68 to 176 degrees F

Timing: 1 hour to 2 weeks

THE CORE DIFFERENCE BETWEEN COLD AND HOT SMOKING

There are two ways to smoke meat that is cold smoking and hot smoking. In cold smoking, meat is cooked between 68 to 86 degrees F until smoked but moist. It is a good choice to smoke meat like chicken breast, steak, beef, pork chops, salmon, and cheese. The cold smoking concern with adding flavor to the meat rather than cooking. Therefore, when the meat is cold smoked, it should be cured, baked or steamed before serving.

On the other hand, hot smoking cooks the meat completely, in addition, to enhance its flavor. Therefore, meat should be a cook until its internal temperature is between 126 to 176 degrees F. Don't let meat temperature reach 185 degrees F as at this temperature, meat shrinks or buckles. Large meat cuts like brisket, ham, ribs and pulled pork turns out great when hot smoked.

THE CORE ELEMENTS OF SMOKING

There are six essential elements of smoking.

1. Wood chips: Chip of woods are used as a fuel either alone or in combination with charcoals. In addition, these chips add fantastic flavor to the meat. Therefore, chips of wood should only be used which suits best to the meat.

2. Smoker: There are basically four choices from which a smoker should be the pick. The choices are an electric smoker, charcoal smoker, gas smoker and pellet smoker. Each has its own advantages and downsides.

3. Smoking time: Smoking time is essential for perfect of meat cuts. It is actually the time when the internal temperature reaches its desired values. It may take 2 hours up to more than two weeks.

4. Meat: The star of the show is meat that needs to be more tender, juicy and flavorful after smoking. Make sure, the meat you sure has fat trimmed from it. In addition, it should complement the wood of chips.

5. Rub: Rubs, mixture or salt and spices, add sweetness and heat to the meat. They should be prepared in such a way that all types of flavor should be balanced in the meat.

6. Mops: Mops or liquid is often used during smoking meat. It adds a little bit flavor to the meat and maintains tenderness and moisture throughout the smoking process.

THE BASIC PREPARATIONS FOR SMOKING MEAT

CHOOSING SMOKER

The major and foremost step is to choose a smoker. You can invest in any type of the smoker: charcoal smoker, gas smoker or an electric smoker. A charcoal smoker runs for a long time and maintain steadier heat in the smoker and give meat pure flavors. A good choice for beginner cook for smoking meat is a gas smoker where there is no need to monitor temperature but it comes with a downside that meat won't have much flavor compared to charcoal. On the other hand, the simplest, easiest and popular smoker is an electric smoker. Cooking with electric smoker involves only two-step: turn it on, put meat in it and walk away. Read more details about smokers in the section "type of smokers".

CHOOSING FUEL

Wood chips add a unique flavor to the meat, therefore, select that wood chips that would enhance the taste of meat. Some wood of chips have a stronger flavor, some have mild while others are just enough to be alone for smoking. Check out the section titled "types of smoker wood" to get to know and decide chips of wood that will complement your meat.

TYPE OF SMOKING METHOD

You have two choices to smoke meat, either using wet smoking, dry smoking, liquid smoke or water smoking. Read the section "The core difference between cold and hot smoking" to find out differences between each. In addition, go through smoking meat portion in the section "the difference between barbecuing a meat and smoking it".

SOAKING CHIPS OF WOOD

Wood chips need to soak in order to last longer for fueling smoking. The reason is dry wood that burns quickly and this means, adding fuel to the smoker which can result in dry smoked meat. There isn't any need of using wood chips when smoking for a shorter time. Prepare wood chips by soaking them in water for at least 4 hours before starting smoking. Then drain chips and wrap and seal them in an aluminium foil. Use toothpick or fork for poking holes into the wood chips bag.

SET SMOKER

Each type of smoker have its own way to start smoking. For wood or charcoal smoker, first, light up half of the charcoals and wait until their flame goes down. Then add remaining charcoal and wood chips if using. Wait they are lighted and giving heat completely, then push charcoal aside and place meat on the other side of grilling grate. This is done to make sure that meat is indirectly smoked over low heat. Continue adding charcoal and/or soaked wood chips into the smoker.

For gas/propane or electric smoker, just turn it on according to manufacturer guideline and then add soaked wood chips into chip holder and fill water receptacle if a smoker has one. Either make use of the incorporated thermostat or buy your own to monitor the internal temperature of the smoker. When smoker reaches to desired preheated temperature, add meat to it.

SELECTING MEAT FOR SMOKING

Choose the type of meat which tastes good with a smoky flavor. Following meat goes well for smoking.

Beef: ribs, brisket and corned beef.

Pork: spare ribs, roast, shoulder, and ham.

Poultry: whole chicken, whole turkey, and big game hens.

Seafood: Salmon, scallops, trout, and lobster.

GETTING MEAT READY

Prepare meat according to the recipe. Sometimes meat is cured, marinated or simply seasoned with the rub. These preparation methods ensure smoked meat turn out flavorful, tender and extremely juicy.

Brine is a solution to treating poultry, pork or ham. It involves dissolving brine ingredients in water poured into a huge container and then adding meat to it. Then let soak for at least 8 hours and after that, rinse it well and pat dry before you begin smoking.

Marinate treat beef or briskets and add flavors to it. It's better to make deep cuts in meat to let marinate ingredients deep into it. Drain meat or smoke it straightaway.

Rubs are commonly used to treat beef, poultry or ribs. They are actually a combination of salt and many spices, rubbed generously all over the meat. Then the meat is left to rest for at least 2 hours or more before smoking it.

Before smoking meat, make sure it is at room temperature. This ensures meat is cooked evenly and reach its internal temperature at the end of smoking time.

PLACING MEAT INTO THE SMOKER

Don't place the meat directly over heat into the smoker because the main purpose of smoking is cooking meat at low temperature. Set aside your fuel on one side of the smoker and place meat on the other side and let cook.

Smoking time: The smoking time of meat depends on the internal temperature. For this, use a meat thermometer and insert it into the thickest part of the meat. The smoking time also varies with the size of meat. Check recipes to determine the exact smoking time for the meat.

BASTING MEAT

Some recipes call for brushing meat with thin solutions, sauces or marinade. This step not only makes meat better in taste, it also helps to maintain moisture in meat through the smoking process. Read recipe to check out if basting is necessary.

Taking out meat: When the meat reaches its desired internal temperature, remove it from the smoker. Generally, poultry should be removed from smoker when its internal temperature reaches to 165 degrees F. For ground meats, ham, and pork, the internal temperature should be 160 degrees F. 145 degrees F is the internal temperature for chops, roast, and steaks.

Conclusion

As you can see from these recipes, the world of smoking is only as limited as your imagination! Sweet, savory, vegetable, mineral, meat- you can smoke almost anything. As you get more comfortable with these recipes, feel free to start experimenting on your own. The basic principles hold true, but your own taste buds can drive you. Good luck, and happy smoking!